Cub Quiz

by Nicholas Spencer

(l)Chris Wallace/Alamy; (r)Aditya Singh/age fotostock

I see little eyes.

I see little ears.

(l)Chris Wallace/Alamy;
(r)Aditya Singh/age fotostock

I see little teeth.

I see little noses.

(l)John E Marriott/All Canada Photos/Getty Images; (r)Roland Weihrauch/Photoshot

I see little tails.

I see little paws.

I see little cubs.